HOW TO MAKE MONEY

FROM YOUR SPARE TIME

RITA STOREY

FRANKLIN WATTS
LONDON • SYDNEY

Franklin Watts
First published in Great Britain in 2017 by
The Watts Publishing Group

Credits
Series editor: Sarah Peutrill
Editor: Sarah Ridley
Packaged by Storeybooks
Series design: Rocket Design (East Anglia) Ltd
Cover design: Peter Scoulding

ISBN 978 1 4451 5284 4

Printed in China

MIX
Paper from
responsible sources
FSC® C104740
FSC
www.fsc.org

Picture acknowledgements
The publisher would like to thank the following for permission to reproduce their photos: Alan Fisher 29 (bottom);
Shutterstock/Konstantin Aksenov 3 (top), 12 (bottom); Shutterstock/Aleutie 4 (bottom); Shutterstock/Angelina Dimitrova
14 (bottom); Shutterstock/Doremi 16 (bottom left); Shutterstock/filborg 7 (bottom), 20 (bottom left), 23 (bottom left),
24 (bottom); Shutterstock/geertweggen 16 (top middle); Shutterstock/Marius Godoi 17; Shutterstock/Jenter 19 (top);
Shutterstock/Matej Kastelic 5 (bottom); Shutterstock/Lapina 23 (bottom left); Shutterstock/LilKar 16 (top right); Shutterstock/
littleny 11; Shutterstock/lu-photo 16 (top left); Shutterstock/naum 18 (top); Shutterstock/NotionPic 2 (left), 23 (bottom right);
Shutterstock/Paccione 14 (top); Shutterstock/Phase4Studios 22 (bottom middle); Shutterstock/Portare fortuna 17 (top), 22
(top); Shutterstock/Pretty Vectors 5 (top), 13 (top), 21 (middle), 25 (bottom); Shutterstock/Rattanataipob 7 (top); Shutterstock/
Neda Sadreddin 6 (centre bottom), 28; Shutterstock/siridhata 16 (bottom right), 19 (bottom), 23 (top), 27; Shutterstock/
subarashii21 5 (middle), 6 (except centre bottom), 10, 18 (bottom), 19 (middle), 20, 26 (top), 29 (top); Shutterstock/topimages
21; Shutterstock/VGstockstudio 22 (bottom left), 22 (bottom right); Shutterstock vector 15; Shutterstock/vladwel 2 (right), 24
(top and middle), 26 (bottom); Shutterstock/Ria Wonder 3 (bottom), 4 (top); Shutterstock/Zoom Team 12 (top).

Every attempt has been made to clear copyright. Should there be any inadvertent omission please apply to
the publisher for rectification.

Franklin Watts
An imprint of
Hachette Children's Group
Part of The Watts Publishing Group
Carmelite House
50 Victoria Embankment
London EC4Y 0DZ

An Hachette UK Company
www.hachette.co.uk

www.franklinwatts.co.uk

If you create a very profitable business you will need
to pay tax on the money you earn. It is important to
keep records of all your sales as well as the receipts
for the things you buy to run the business.
Tax laws vary from country to country. If your
business begins to make money, find out about
your business responsibilities.

Read the 'Stay Safe' instructions
throughout this book and follow the
advice to use the Internet safely.

CONTENTS

Why start a business? 4

The idea 6
    Business idea 1: Daisy Roots plant sales

Research 8

Target marketing 10

Creating a brand 12

Pricing for profit 13

Production 16

Selling 18

The Internet 20
    Business idea 2: mycrazyhobbyclub.com blog and vlog

Use your skills 22
    Business idea 3: Outdoor Pet Pix photography

Offer a service 24
    Business idea 4: Sparkly Cars cleaning service

Get SMART 26

Work part-time 27

Now what? 28

Business jargon/Further information 30

Index 32

WHY START A BUSINESS?

Someone who sets up their own business rather than working for someone else is called an entrepreneur. Owning your own business means that you are the boss. Being the boss of a business that focuses on something you enjoy doing in your spare time allows you to turn your private passion into a profit.

What is a business?

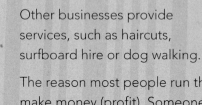

GOODS

Some businesses make things (goods) that customers buy in the shops or online, such as handmade products or cakes, clothes or sports equipment.

Other businesses provide services, such as haircuts, surfboard hire or dog walking.

The reason most people run their own business is to make money (profit). Someone who builds a business around a favourite pastime may want to make as much money as they can from all their hard work.

SERVICES

However, many people who turn a pastime into a business create a lifestyle business. This is a business where making money is not the only goal. The business owner may be happy to earn just enough to fund a certain way of life. For example, a passionate surfer might set up a surfboard hire company next to a great surfing beach while a dog lover might start a dog-walking business, so that they can spend every day walking dogs.

To start a lifestyle business you need:

✓ A firm idea of what lifestyle suits you.

✓ A creative idea about how to use your passion to provide a product or service that other people will be prepared to buy.

✓ Money to pay for all the things you need to get the business started. These are called start-up costs.

✓ Customers or consumers who will buy the product or service. For your business to make money there must be enough customers who want to buy the products or service at the price you are charging.

✓ A lot of energy and enthusiasm.

Starting your own business at an early age can have drawbacks. Opening a bank account and selling through online websites will mean you will need an adult to help you. Do you know anyone who has started their own business? Is there a teacher at your school who is interested in supporting young entrepreneurs? These people may act as your mentors to help you through the process.

Starting a lifestyle business in your spare time will be a lot of hard work but if the reward is getting paid for something you already love doing, it will make the hard work worthwhile.

Pages 7, 20, 23 and 24 have made-up examples of four different types of business. Read about how to set them up in order to create businesses that could make money from your spare time.

THE IDEA

To set up a lifestyle business based on an activity that you already enjoy in your spare time, you'll need to identify a product or service within that activity that people will be prepared to pay for. Entrepreneurs who have passion are often the most successful.

Business model

You may decide to run your business alone and be a sole trader. If you have a friend who shares your passion you could form a partnership.

SOLE TRADER

✓ Total control of what you do.

✓ Total responsibility.

✓ Keep all the profits.

✓ Responsible for all the losses.

PARTNERSHIP

✓ Shared control of the business.

✓ Shared responsibility.

✓ Shared profits.

✓ Shared losses.

CORPORATION

Larger businesses, called corporations, have shareholders. Shareholders put money into a business by buying shares and are rewarded with a share in the profit.

BUSINESS IDEA 1
Daisy Roots plant sales

You and a friend are passionate about wildlife and the environment. You live in a city and you love gardening.

The business idea

To grow and sell plants that will encourage birds and insects into city gardens. To grow the seedlings in eco-pots. To make your plants stand out they will be displayed in old shoes or boots.

Think carefully about your idea. Can you see any drawbacks?

Problems and solutions

You do not have much money to start up the business.

Keep the business costs very low by making your own eco-pots from recycled newspaper or cardboard tubes.

Caring for the plants takes up a lot of time.

Work as a partnership so that you can share the plant care.

The business is very seasonal.

Plant seeds a few weeks apart to ensure you have a continuous supply of plants to sell. Be prepared to have periods of time when you will not be making money.

RESEARCH

It is sensible to do some research before starting up a business. It could save you time and money in the long run, as if the research shows that not many people like your product or service, you can start again and think of another idea.

Product research

Find out as much as you can about the product you want to sell. This is called product research.

The Internet

Use the Internet to find out which plants are best for attracting wildlife to city gardens. Wildlife charities and gardening sites, such as the Royal Horticultural Society, are good places to start your research.

Books and magazines

Find out from gardening books and magazines how easy it is to grow insect- and bird-friendly plants.

The competition

Are any of the plants you have identified being sold in local garden centres, markets or supermarkets? How expensive are they?

Another area of research is to find out as much as you can about the market where your products or services can be sold to customers, whether that is an Internet shop, a high street shop, a market or a special event, such as a charity fair. This is called market research.

Types of market research

- Street surveys or questionnaires: asking people questions in person.
- Finding out information by reading books and looking at information online.

Design a questionnaire. Ask friends and neighbours to fill in your questionnaire. Take an adult with you if you are taking your questionnaire outside your home.

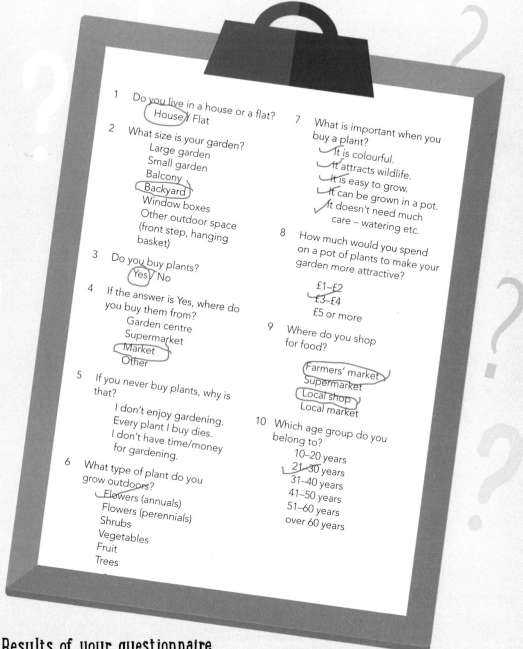

1 Do you live in a house or a flat?
   House / Flat

2 What size is your garden?
   Large garden
   Small garden
   Balcony
   Backyard
   Window boxes
   Other outdoor space
   (front step, hanging
   basket)

3 Do you buy plants?
   Yes / No

4 If the answer is Yes, where do you buy them from?
   Garden centre
   Supermarket
   Market
   Other

5 If you never buy plants, why is that?
   I don't enjoy gardening.
   Every plant I buy dies.
   I don't have time/money for gardening.

6 What type of plant do you grow outdoors?
   Flowers (annuals)
   Flowers (perennials)
   Shrubs
   Vegetables
   Fruit
   Trees

7 What is important when you buy a plant?
   It is colourful.
   It attracts wildlife.
   It is easy to grow.
   It can be grown in a pot.
   It doesn't need much care – watering etc.

8 How much would you spend on a pot of plants to make your garden more attractive?
   £1–£2
   £3–£4
   £5 or more

9 Where do you shop for food?
   Farmers' market
   Supermarket
   Local shop
   Local market

10 Which age group do you belong to?
   10–20 years
   21–30 years
   31–40 years
   41–50 years
   51–60 years
   over 60 years

Results of your questionnaire

Compare the results from several questionnaires. The person who filled in this questionnaire (above) would like to grow colourful plants that attract wildlife. He or she likes plants that are easy to maintain, and that are easy to grow in pots.

From your questionnaire results, you can then identify the group of people who are most likely to buy your plants, what size of home they live in and the size of their garden.

TARGET MARKETING

Businesses rely on their customers for sales and profit. A successful business puts the needs of the customer or consumer at the heart of their business.

Marketing is all the things associated with buying and selling a product and finding customers. When you have identified a market for your products, you can target the marketing to that group.

USPs

Make a list of the things that make your products different or better than your competitors' products. This list is called your USPs – Unique Selling Points. Use your USPs to target potential customers.

USPs for your plants

✓ Good for the local environment – the plants feed birds and insects.

✓ Improve the enjoyment of the customer's garden – attract more bird and insect visitors.

✓ Grown in eco-friendly compost (peat-free/organic).

✓ Kind to the environment – plants grown without use of chemical fertilisers or pesticides.

✓ Attractive – the plants are chosen for their colour and scent.

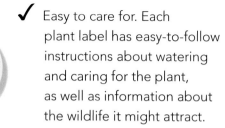

✓ Easy to care for. Each plant label has easy-to-follow instructions about watering and caring for the plant, as well as information about the wildlife it might attract.

✓ Reasonably priced.

These plants will make our boring backyard really colourful.

And attract lots of wildlife hopefully.

The marketing mix

A perfect marketing mix is sometimes called the four Ps: Product, Price, Place and Promotion.

Use the research you have done to target a perfect marketing mix.

PRODUCT

The market research indicates that customers want plants that are:

- Colourful
- Attractive to wildlife
- Easy to grow and look after
- Able to thrive in a container

PRICE

The market research indicates that customers want plants that cost:

- Between £3–£4

(See page 13 for more on pricing.)

PLACE

The market research indicates that customers buy plants from:

- Garden centres
- Farmers' markets
- Local shops

PROMOTION

These are ways to make people aware of your products at the right time by promoting them through:

- Advertising
- Publicity
- Sales promotions

The marketing plan

✓ You are going to sell colourful annual flowers and some longer lasting plants.

✓ The pots of flowers will cost £3. The plants will cost £4.

✓ You will sell the plants at:

- A farmers' market

- A local shop selling organic produce

Both outlets have agreed to stock a few products to see how they sell.

FARMERS' MARKET

CREATING A BRAND

The image that your company and your products have in the market is called your brand. Within a brand you can have lots of different products. When customers recognise your brand and buy from you repeatedly you have created brand loyalty.

Brand image

Decide what image you want to put across to your customer.

A good business name is very important. It can be something memorable or it can describe the business. When you have decided on a name, design a logo to reinforce the ideas behind the business.

The business name could be:

Daisy Roots

Design a plant label that can carry information about the plant, the insects or birds it attracts, your logo as well as instructions on plant care. Keep the text simple – bullet points work well.

Recycle old shoes as plant containers .

Think about how the plants will be displayed. Print out the logo and stick it onto card. Make sure it can be read clearly from a distance.

Talk to the owners of the shop and farmers' market to see where they are thinking of placing the plants for sale. Can you hang a sign nearby or position a pile of leaflets with information about the products?

Can you think of other ways to attract customers to your plants?

PRICING FOR PROFIT

Sensible entrepreneurs want to put their efforts into something that has a good chance of success, so they work out their business costs before they start.

Some will make a business plan, not only working out the start-up costs but also working out a plan for how to develop the business once it has got off the ground. As Daisy Roots is a lifestyle business, you may only need to work out the start-up costs for now – that's the costs involved in making your plant pots ready to sell to customers.

The right price

How you price your products is one way of gaining a bigger share of the market.

A lower price can increase sales but if it is too low it can give the impression of poor quality.

BARGAIN PRICE

A low price in the right place is a bargain.
A low price in the wrong place is cheap.

PRICE CUTS

A higher price can make a product seem desirable.

Flowers and flowering plants are often more expensive to buy at certain times of the year, such as Valentine's Day, Easter and Mother's Day. This is because there is a demand for flowers at this time and customers are prepared to pay more.

Reducing a price can make customers feel that a product has not been popular.

REDUCED

Marketing opportunities

You need to weigh up the pros and cons of marketing opportunities. Many people give plants as Mother's Day, Valentine or Easter gifts. You can increase the price at these times, but if your plants don't sell during the main selling season you may have to sell them at a lower price after the event and make a loss.

Unit cost

It is important to work out exactly what profit you will make from the things you sell.

Calculate the cost of the materials needed to both grow the plants and present them for sale – the seeds, the compost, the pots and the labels.

1 Research the best source of seeds at the cheapest price. You might be able to get a better price if you buy many packets of seed at once, but take care. Seeds have a sell-by date so they may not keep until next year if you buy too many. Do some research – is your local garden centre doing a deal if you buy more than one bag of peat-free compost?

2 How many seeds are sold in each packet? Usually gardeners find that only about half the seeds successfully grow into adult plants. So divide the price of each packet of seeds by half the number of seeds it contains to give you the price of each seed.

3 Divide the price of a bag of peat-free organic compost by the number of pots you can fill from a bag.

4 As you are recycling paper to make the pots, reusing unwanted shoes and boots, from family and friends, to present them in, there are no other cost involved apart from your time. Now add the plant seed and compost costs together to give you the cost of a pot containing a plant.

Profit margin

To calculate your profit margin, take the cost of producing each finished product away from the price you are selling it at.

Direct costs

These are all the things that you need to spend money on in order to make products. The amount of products you make changes the direct costs.

Indirect costs

These are the costs not directly related to the product. The rent of a market stall is an indirect cost. The indirect costs stay the same however many products you make.

Wholesale and retail

If you are selling your plants to a shop, they need to make a profit when they sell them. The shop owner will buy your plants from you for a wholesale price; a lower price than you can charge if you sell direct to customers. The shop owner then charges customers the retail price. The difference between the wholesale and retail prices is the profit for the shop owner.

Sale or return

To avoid the risk of making a loss when products do not sell, shops take items on 'sale or return'. This means that they only pay for the products that they sell and will return any unsold items after a set period of time to the supplier.

Adding value

A plant business is a seasonal business. Plants that flower within a few months of being sown are called annuals. Usually gardeners plant annuals in spring and they flower in the summer. Some plants, such as biennial or perennials, take more than one year to grow from seed but usually last a lot longer in the garden. If you look after a plant for longer before selling it, you can ask a higher price. So grow annuals alongside other plants to ensure you have plants to sell for many months of the year, and at different prices.

PRODUCTION

To get your business idea off the ground, you need some products to sell. For the Daisy Roots business, this means having plants to sell. Decide on two or three types of plant to start off your business.

CHIVES

SUNFLOWERS

POPPIES

This type of business is a low-cost start-up but you will still need a small amount of money to begin.

Raising money

Assets are money or things that you already have that can be sold to raise money.

Money

Do you have any savings that you could use to start your business?

Other assets

You can sell clothes in good condition on the Internet through online auction sites such as ebay and Gumtree.

Ask an adult to help you run a car boot sale or garage sale to sell old clothes or toys in good condition.

Can you make money by doing jobs for members of your family or for friends? Ideas: you could wash cars, weed front gardens, bake cakes, walk dogs, look after pets, wash windows.

Family and friends may be prepared to give set amounts of money to start your business.

We can borrow a trowel for now.

My dad has a Sunday newspaper so we can use that to make eco-pots once he has read it.

We still need to buy seeds and compost.

The production process

Once you have enough money to buy seeds and compost, you need to create some products to sell. This is called the production process.

What to do:

1 Make up eco plant pots by folding recycled paper (see page 31 for a YouTube video that can help you), or use old egg boxes or the inside of kitchen rolls with one end folded over.

2 Buy a bag of peat-free organic seed compost.

3 Following instructions on the seed packets, carefully plant the seeds.

4 Once the seeds have sprouted, look after the seedlings until they have grown into plants of a suitable size to sell. You will need to re-pot them into larger eco-pots filled with all-uses peat-free organic compost as they grow. Re-pot the fully grown plant into a boot or shoe for display.

ECO-POTS

The time between the start and the finish of the production process is your lead time. This is the time when no money is coming in but you will need to spend money. Money going in and out of the business is called cash flow. Predicting when money is going to come in and go out is called a cash flow forecast.

SELLING

At some point, all entrepreneurs have to become salespeople, convincing other people to buy their products or services, and selling themselves to the outside world as a believable business person. It can be nerve-racking but no-one is born able to sell – it is a skill you learn from watching other people.

A pitch

In a competitive market, customers want to know why they should buy your product over any other. You'll need to practise your pitch, a brief presentation during which you tell interested customers or retailers the key facts about your products and your business aims. If you are running a lifestyle business, this shouldn't prove too difficult as you will already know a lot about your product and feel passionate about it. Keep to the point – make your pitch no longer than two minutes long.

✓ How well do you know your product? Do the research. A pitch is easy if you know the facts.

✓ If a retailer is interested in stocking your products they will want to discuss pricing. Can you remember the unit price? If you agree to a price that is too low you may not make any profit.

✓ Mentally tick off a list of the key points, your USPs (see page 10), as you present your pitch.

✓ Practise in front of a mirror, or practise delivering the presentation to a friend.

✓ Try to look confident. This is not easy but will get better the more times you do it.

Tell people about the benefits of planting your chosen plants in their gardens.

✓ Attracting more wildlife to their garden.

✓ Creating more colour in their garden.

✓ Being able to enjoy beautiful scented plants in their garden.

✓ Growing plants that they can cut for flower arrangements indoors.

✓ Supporting wildlife by growing more of the plants that give them food.

When you have delivered your pitch, listen to people's comments (the feedback) and try to offer solutions.

I don't have time to water plants.

We sell this plant because bees love it and it only needs watering occasionally.

Tax

If you create a very profitable business you will need to pay tax on the money you earn. Whether or not your business earns enough to pay tax, it is important to keep good records of every sale you make, as well as all the receipts for things (seeds and compost) that you bought in order to run the business.

Tax laws vary from country to country. If your business begins to make money, check out the rules regarding tax. Businesses often employ an accountant to do this for them.

THE INTERNET

Whatever your interest, hobby, sport or craft, you can reach like-minded people who share your passion through the Internet. Blogs and vlogs (video blogs) are set up to build a relationship between the blogger or vlogger and the reader. Alternatively, e-commerce websites are online shops to sell your products. Learn how to use the Internet to support your lifestyle business.

Bloggers build a community of followers by interacting with people who share their interests. A blog sharing an interest in anything from make-up to gaming, chess to fishing can become a business opportunity.

If you have an unusual interest you could set up a niche blog site. You could use it to attract a number of followers from all over the world and, you never know, you could convert more people to the thing you love.

BUSINESS IDEA 2

mycrazyhobbyclub.com blog and vlog

You like making art out of bottle tops. Your friends think it is a crazy hobby.

The business idea

To set up a blog and a vlog site about making art out of bottle tops. Make videos and write a blog about the different stages of making the pictures.
At the same time, invite other people with crazy hobbies to add content to the site.

What to do:

✓ Create a blog website or a YouTube channel.

✓ Make videos showing how you create the pictures.

✓ Take step-by step photos.

✓ Upload the videos via YouTube or Vimeo.

✓ Upload the written content and photos to your blog site.

Invite people to share information about their unusual hobbies. Before you know it you will have a community of crazy hobbyists.

Challenge people to create bigger and better pictures or sculptures. Set up an online gallery.

How to make money from the site

- If enough people follow your blog, manufacturers may send you products to review. To increase the number of followers, link to Facebook, Twitter and Instagram. Tweet about your blog. Send photos via Instagram. Sign up to Google Analytics (a service offered by Google that tracks website traffic). Update your Facebook page regularly to keep followers up-to-date with what you are doing. Keep adding new content to your site.

! Stay safe

Blogs and vlogs are a brilliant way to interact with a large number of people, but make sure you protect yourself from people who misuse the Internet.

- Do not use your real name for your blog or reveal information that lets people know your location.

- Do not include email addresses or mobile phone numbers.

USE YOUR SKILLS

Do you have a reasonably good camera?

Do you know how to use your camera?

Do you like animals?

Do people admire your photographs?

If you answer YES to these questions then using your skill as a photographer to set up a pet photography business may be right for you. People love their pets and many are willing to pay for a good pet portrait.

Research

Look on the Internet and elsewhere to see what other photographers are doing.

Check what services the photographers are offering and note down the fees that professional photographers charge.

Persuade friends or members of your family to pose with their pet. Take different types of portrait photograph to try out ideas. Ask permission to use the finished photo portraits on your blog or vlog site to promote your business.

Discuss their pet's personality.

Is the animal funny, beautiful, regal or aristocratic? Think how you could bring out their personality in a photograph and try out different styles.

Colour posed portrait

Cute, colour portrait

Black-and-white posed portrait

Market research

Show your photographs to as many people as you can. Ask them which pictures they like best. Ask them how much they would be prepared to pay for a similar photo.

If one photograph stands out then it may be a good idea to specialise. Use your special talent with a particular style of portrait photography to advertise your skills.

Which is your favourite photo?

I love the black-and -white one.

BUSINESS IDEA 3
Outdoor Pet Pix

The business idea

To start a photography business that takes high quality black-and-white portraits of pets and their owners outdoors.

Where to advertise

- The local veterinary practice or pet shop – ask if you can put up a poster or leave some flyers.

- Local parks – is there a café where you can leave flyers or put up a poster?

- Start a blog about the business (see page 20).

- Set up an online gallery. Ask your clients for permission to use their photographs.

- Form a Facebook group of pet owners.

- Enter photography competitions. Before you do this, make sure you have the pet owners' permission to use the photos in this way.

OFFER A SERVICE

It is often very difficult to find a regular part-time job that fits in with school hours and homework. There are laws that limit the hours you can work and the types of job you can do while you are under 16, so check first. Instead, why not offer a service that fits in with your spare time?

Dog walking, car cleaning, housework, oven cleaning, cooking and babysitting are all service jobs that can be fitted in alongside school hours and homework.

BUSINESS IDEA 4

Sparkly Cars

You asked local people what job they hate doing at the weekend. Cleaning the car was high on the list. You have looked at prices for car washing services at local supermarkets and other car washes and think you can provide a good service at a cheaper price.

The business idea

To offer a low-cost hand car wash and vacuum service at the weekend if people sign up for several weeks.

Clean a car for a family member. Time how long it took. Do you need any supplies to do the job? Use the information on page 14 to work out an hourly rate.

1 Design a leaflet with information about your business. Include a price list for different sizes of car.

Give the leaflet to people you know first. They can be used for market research. Ask them for feedback.

2 When you are confident, begin to market your business. Do a leaflet drop in your local area. Include an incentive to get customers to sign up.

3 You will need a bank account to pay cheques into. Keep records of what you get paid.

Incentives

Introductory offer

Offer one trial wash and vacuum at a low price to encourage customers to sign up.

Loyalty

Design a loyalty card. Reward loyalty by offering a free car clean after nine visits. That gives customers ten car washes for the price of nine.

Stay safe

Set the business up with a friend. That way you will not have to visit the houses alone. Let someone know where you are at all times.

GET SMART

It is always useful in a business to have goals to work towards. These can be short-, medium- or long-term goals. In the short term your goal may be to process orders on the same day that you receive them – in the medium term it may be to increase your product range in the next three months and a long-term goal might be to increase your profit by a certain amount within three years.

Goals should follow the acronym (an abbreviation made from the initial letters of other words and pronounced as a word) SMART.

SMART

Specific   Define each individual goal. So, rather than loosely aiming to make more profit, aim to increase profits by say 10 per cent in a year.

Measurable   Keep careful records so that you know if you have achieved your goals.

Agreed   If you are working in partnership with someone else, make sure you are both working towards the same goals.

Realistic   If a goal is unachievable you will be disheartened very quickly. Set a goal that is just outside what you think is achievable.

Timed   Set a time frame for each achievement and review the goals when the time comes.

This is what the short-, medium- and long-term SMART goals might look like for Sparkly Cars.

Short term To have 20 regular clients in the next three months.

Medium term To expand the range of services offered to include a full cleaning service by the end of next year.

Long term To increase the profit of the company to £5,000 in year 4.

WORK PART-TIME

Getting a job to fit in with school work can be difficult, but it can have a lot of benefits.

Benefits of working part-time

✓ You will learn to work as part of a team.

✓ It will teach you to be good at timekeeping and to understand why being on time is important when people rely on you.

✓ It will teach you about managing your time so that you can fit in school work and paid work.

✓ It will make you more responsible.

✓ It will build your confidence.

✓ It may help you get a reference for further education or job applications.

✓ It may lead to a full-time job.

✓ You will earn money.

How to find a job

Ask friends and family if they know of anyone looking for help.

Ask around the local area. Shops often need extra help at weekends when they are at their busiest. If you live in an area visited by tourists, short-term jobs may be available at the busiest times.

If you want to gain skills while helping others, you could become a volunteer. Wildlife trusts, veterinary surgeries, riding stables and charity shops may welcome reliable volunteers. Although you are unlikely to receive any payment, some organisations offer benefits in return, such as a riding lesson in return for mucking out the stables. On top of this, it can be very satisfying to be a volunteer, can lead to new friendships with people who share your interests and may even give you vital work experience to help you get a job or successfully apply for a course in the future.

NOW WHAT?

Whether you have a lifestyle business based on a favourite activity or are using your spare time to make money, there comes a point where you need to look at what you have achieved and make some decisions about where the business is going.

✓ You have created a successful business

If your business is a lifestyle business, are these statements true?

- I have time to pursue my favourite activity and make money too.
- It allows me to meet other like-minded people.
- It is fun.

If your business is a service business, can you think of ways to make more profit?

Daisy Roots Think of ways to attract publicity. At the farmers' market make big insects out of papier mâché to make your stall stand out.

mycrazyhobbyclub.com Run a competition for who can invent the craziest hobby or make the biggest bottle-top sculpture.

Outdoor Pet Pix Puppies grow very quickly. Offer a photo-a-month package deal for puppy owners to document the first six months of their puppy's life.

THEN

It is up to you! One of the joys of being in business is that the decisions about what to do next are yours to take and are not in the hands of an employer. Lifestyle businesses are not all about profit even if you are successfully running a business based on your favourite activity.

✗ Your business is not making money

If your business is a lifestyle business, are these statements true?

- I no longer have time to pursue my favourite activity.

- Making a profit has stopped me enjoying the company of other people who share my interests.

- It is no longer fun.

If you have set up a service business using the spare time that you have and it is not successful, do you know why your business idea did not work?

- Was your product or service too expensive?

- Was your product or service too cheap for you to make money?

- Could you increase the price?

- Could you lower the price to increase the amount of customers?

- Could you offer any additional services?

THEN

If running a business has taken the enjoyment out of your hobby then you may be better using the skills you have learnt and applying them to another business.

If it is a service business, can you see another, better business opportunity? Entrepreneurs are always looking for new business ideas.

Take all the lessons you have learned, go back to page 4 and start all over again! Very few entrepreneurs achieve success with the first business they set up. What they have in common is that they refuse to let it put them off trying again.

'IF YOU CAN DREAM IT, YOU CAN DO IT.'

Walt Disney (1901–1966), cartoon and film producer and businessman

29

BUSINESS JARGON

A glossary of business words and expressions

A

advertising Activities, such as displaying posters, placing adverts or broadcasting adverts on TV, that attract attention to products or services.

annual A plant that performs its lifecycle within one growing season.

assets In business, money, property or things of value that are owned by the business.

B

blog A website set up to encourage and interact with its followers, or an article posted on a website.

brand The image of a product a business creates to set their product apart from other similar products (high-class, luxury, low-cost etc).

business An organisation that makes goods or provides services, and sells them for money.

C

cash flow Money going into and out of a business.

company Any type of business that trades goods or services.

compost A mixture of soil and rotted down plant material used to grow seeds or plants or increase goodness in the soil.

consumer In business, the person who buys a product or service.

customer Someone who buys products or services.

D

direct costs Costs linked to making a product or delivering a service. Direct costs are higher when more products are made or services delivered.

E

e-commerce (electronic commerce) Buying and selling over the Internet.

entrepreneur Someone who starts a business, taking on the responsibility for the risks and rewards.

F

fertiliser A substance, natural or chemical, added to the soil to make plants grow better.

G

goal An aim or ambition.

goods A physical product, such as a cake or a car, that can be sold to supply a want or a need.

I

incentive Something that encourages someone to buy or do something.

indirect costs Costs not directly linked to the product. Indirect costs have to be paid whether or not products sell.

L

lead time The time it takes from design to a finished product.

lifestyle business A business set up to allow the owner to enjoy a particular lifestyle.

loyalty In business, when customers buy again.

M

market A place where goods or services are traded for money, such as a shop or a website.

market research Gathering information about the market for a product or service.

marketing All the activities needed to sell a product or service, including advertising, promotion and sales.

mentor A person with experience who acts as an advisor to someone with less experience.

O

online gallery site A website where you can set up an online shop to sell vintage, handmade and unusual craft products or paintings.

organic Here, compost produced without the use of artificial chemicals.

P

partnership A business owned by two or more people.

peat A type of non-sustainable soil material created by plants rotting down in damp conditions for hundreds of years.

perennial A plant with a lifecycle that may last several years.

pesticide A substance used to kill insect or other animal pests.

pitch A presentation summarising a business idea. Also, a place to set up a market stall.

product An item that has been manufactured for sale.

profit The amount of money left over once costs have been deducted from sales.

profit margin The percentage of profit after costs have been deducted.

promotion Ways of letting people know that your business and products exist.

publicity Giving out information in different ways, such as TV appearances or adverts, in order to attract attention to a product, person or event.

Q

questionnaire A list of questions used to collect information about a specific subject, product or service.

R

research To find out more information about something.

retail price The price paid by a customer to the seller of a product.

S

sale or return When products are given to retailers to offer for sale and they only pay for those that sell, returning any unsold products.

seasonal Relating to a time of the year.

seedling A young plant.

services Activities such as banking or hairdressing that can be sold to customers.

sole trader One person owning a business.

start-up costs The one-off costs of starting a new business.

stock The goods or products that are ready to sell (stored in a shop or warehouse).

T

tax A contribution to the costs of government paid by earners and businesses.

U

unit cost The cost of making a single product.

upcycle Reuse something in such a way that it creates a product of greater value than the original.

USPs (Unique Selling Points) The things that make a company or a product stand out from its competitors.

V

vlog A video blog.

W

wholesale price The price paid by a retailer to a manufacturer of goods.

Further information

https://www.youtube.com/watch?v=EblQj_pZFlQ

A video of an inspirational talk given by Gabrielle Jordan Williams, a young entrepreneur who started her own jewellery business.

https://www.youtube.com/watch?v=IP5Fa6A5IFM

Instructional video showing how to make a variety of different eco-pots for seedlings.

https://www.lynda.com/articles/start-a-blog-kids-heres-how

A blog about how to start up a blog.

https://iwantmyname.com/services/blog-hosting/blogger-custom-domain

A website that shows you how to set up your own domain.

Note to parents and teachers: every effort has been made by the Publishers to ensure that these websites are suitable for children, that they are of the highest educational value, and that they contain no inappropriate or offensive material. However, because of the nature of the Internet, it is impossible to guarantee that the contents of these sites will not be altered.

We strongly advise that Internet access is supervised by a responsible adult.

INDEX

advertising 11, 23
assets 16

blogs 20–23
branding 12–13
business, closing down a 29

cash flow 17
companies 6
cost, unit 14
costs 7, 13–16
costs, start up 5, 7, 13, 16

Disney, Walt 29

e-commerce 20

goals 4, 26

ideas, business
    Daisy Roots plant sales 7, 12–19, 28
    My crazy hobby club blog 20–21, 28
    Outdoor Pet Pix photography business
        22–23, 28
    Sparkly Cars car wash 24–26
incentives 25

logos 12

marketing 10–11, 13, 25, 28
marketing mix 11
mentors 5
monetise, ways to 21
money, raising 16

partnerships 6–7, 26
pitch, preparing a 18–19
plans, business 13
pricing 5, 10–11, 13–15, 18, 25, 27, 29
production process 16–17
profit margin 15
promotions, sales 11

questionnaires 8, 9

records, keeping 19, 25, 26
research,
    market 8–9, 11, 22–23, 25
    product 8

shareholders 6
SMART 26
social media, using 20-21, 23

tax 19
traders, sole 6

USPs (Unique Selling Points) 10, 18
upcycling 12

vlogs 20–22
volunteering 27

work, part-time 24, 27

YouTube 17, 21

These are the list of contents for each title in the How to make money series.

How to make money from cooking and baking

Why start a business? · Finding a business idea · Finding the right product · Try things out · The right price · A healthy image · Planning · Money, money, money · Making the snacks · Cooking blogs and vlogs · Baking for money · Baking for charity · Have you thought of this? · Promotion

How to make money from your computer

Why start a business? · Selling on the Internet · Create a brand · Blogs and vlogs · Review blogs · Showcase your talent · Crazy stuff · Ways to monetise · Making money from apps or games · Money, money, money · Selling computer services

How to make money from upcycling

Why start a business? · Product design · The market · Marketing · Branding · Selling on the Internet · How to sell at a craft fair · An upcycling blog or vlog · Production · Inventions · People, planet, profit · Running your business · Setting up a website

How to make money from your spare time

Why start a business? · The idea · Research · Target marketing · Creating a brand · Pricing · Production · Selling · The Internet · Use your skills · Offer a service · Get SMART · Work part-time